FREYA

NORSE GODDESS OF LOVE

by Tammy Gagne

Content Consultant
Lauren Poyer
Department of Scandinavian Studies
University of Washington
Seattle, WA

CAPSTONE PRESS
a capstone imprint

Snap Books are published by Capstone Press,
1710 Roe Crest Drive, North Mankato, Minnesota 56003
www.capstonepub.com

Library of Congress Cataloging-in-Publication Data
Names: Gagne, Tammy, author.
Title: Freya : Norse goddess of love / by Tammy Gagne. Description: 1st Ed. | North Mankato, MN : Capstone, 2019. | Series: Snap Books. Legendary goddesses Identifiers: LCCN 2019004856| ISBN 9781543574159 (hardcover) | ISBN 9781543575552 (pbk.) | ISBN 9781543574197 (ebook pdf) Subjects: LCSH: Freya (Norse deity)—Juvenile literature. | Frigg (Norse deity)—Juvenile literature. | Goddesses, Norse—Juvenile literature. Classification: LCC BL870.F48 G34 2019 | DDC 293/.2114—dc23 LC record available at https://lccn.loc.gov/2019004856

Editorial Credits
Michelle Parkin, editor
Bobbie Nuytten, designer
Svetlana Zhurkin, media researcher
Katy LaVigne, production specialist

Image Credits
Alamy: Claudine Klodien, 27, Ivy Close Images, 13, Photo 12, 28, Pictures Now, 10, Science History Images, 9, The History Collection, 14; Mary Evans Picture Library: cover, 21 (top), Interfoto/Sammlung Rauch, 25; Newscom: Album/British Library, 5; Shutterstock: Danny Smythe, 21 (bottom), Galina Barskaya, 29, Jamen Percy, 20, lacostique, 22, Matias Del Carmine, 18 (top, middle, bottom right), NNNMMM, 18 (bottom left), 19, Ravi_sunlight, 6, Reinhold Leitner, 12, TuiPhotoEngineer, 26

Illustrations by Alessandra Fusi
Design Elements by Shutterstock

All internet sites appearing in back matter were available and accurate when this book was sent to press.

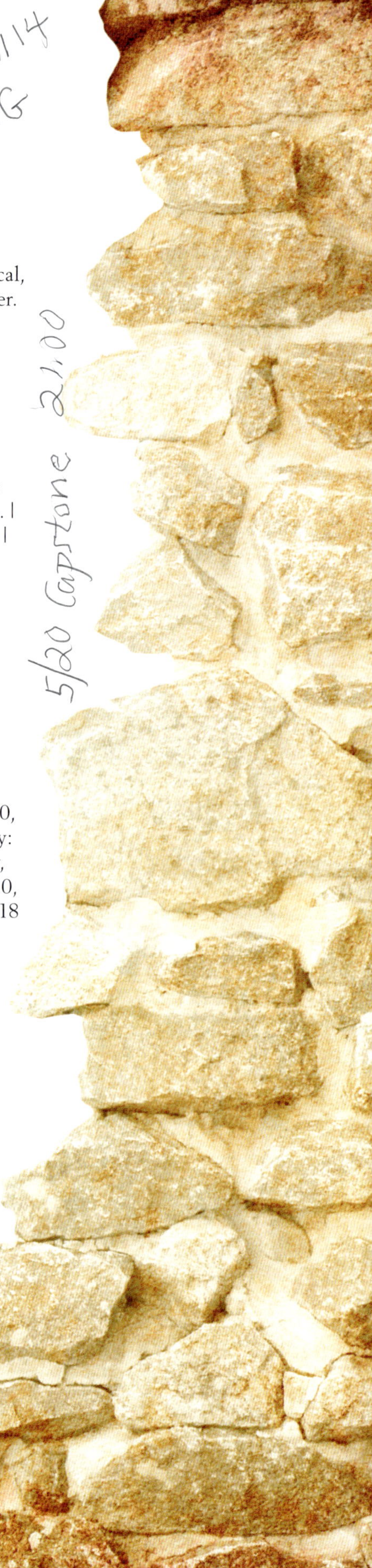

Printed and bound in the USA.
PA70

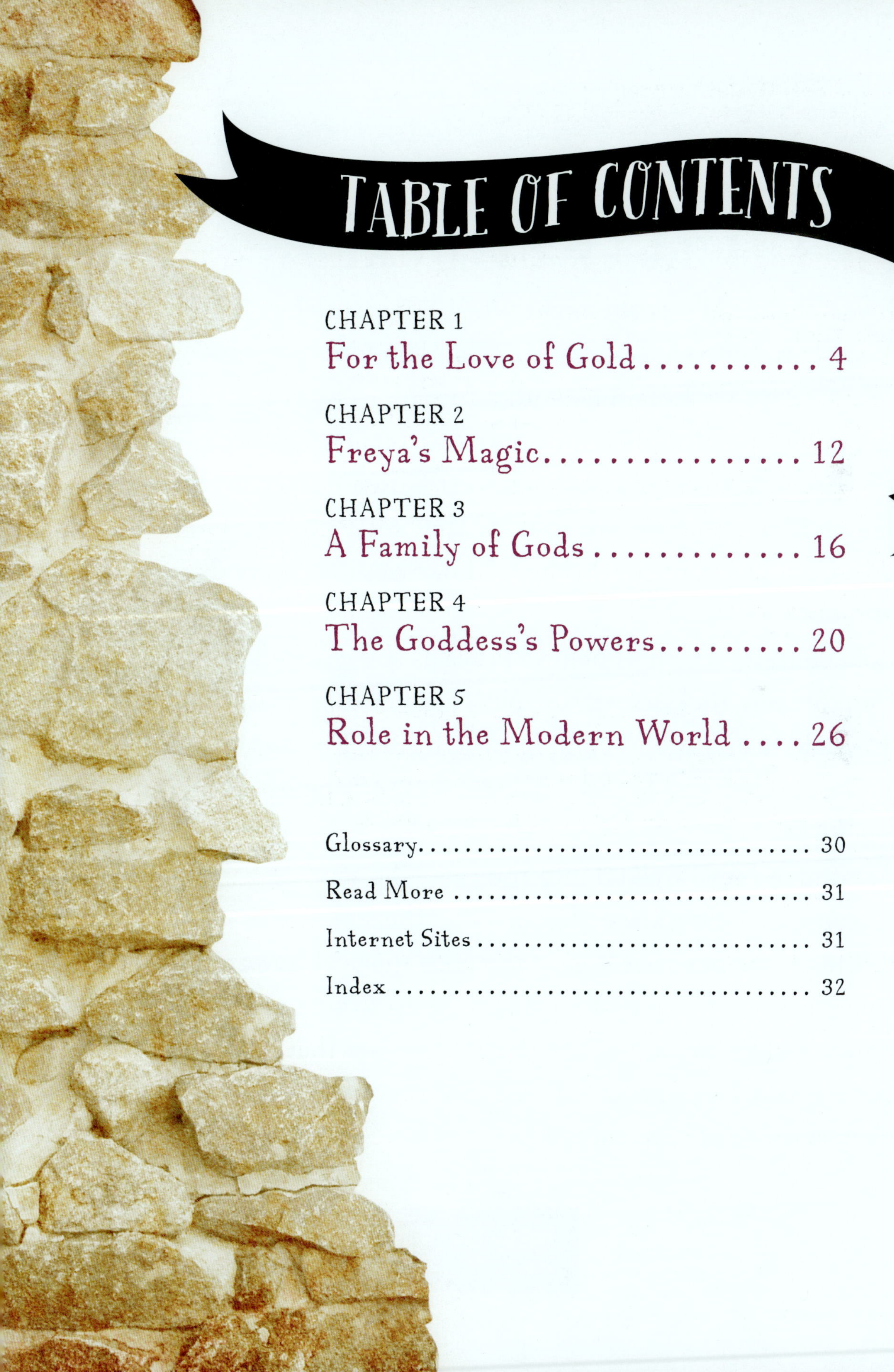

TABLE OF CONTENTS

Chapter 1

FOR THE LOVE OF GOLD

It was the middle of the night when Freya snuck out of Asgard on foot. All the other gods and goddesses were asleep—except for Loki. The god of mischief saw Freya leave and decided to follow her. Snow was falling as they made their way through fields and over a frozen river. What could be so important to draw the Norse goddess of love from her home at this hour? Loki was determined to find out.

Loki continued to trail behind Freya as she reached a group of large rocks. A narrow path led her to a cave. Freya could hear a sound coming from inside. *Tap. Tap. Tap.* The goddess had found what she was searching for—a **forge**.

As soon as Freya walked into the cave, she saw Brisingamen. The necklace gleamed like the sun. It was beautiful. Some believed it gave the gods magical powers. Brisingamen was made by four dwarfs, who stood nearby. Freya wanted to buy it, but the dwarfs told her that it wasn't for sale. Freya persisted. She told them she would pay any amount of silver or gold.

forge—a place where metal is melted and molded into various objects

The dwarfs said they had enough silver and gold. Finally they suggested a trade. If Freya stayed with them in the cave for four days and nights, she could have the necklace. She hated the idea. But her desire for the necklace was strong. She agreed to their terms.

Freya bargained with the dwarfs for the precious necklace.

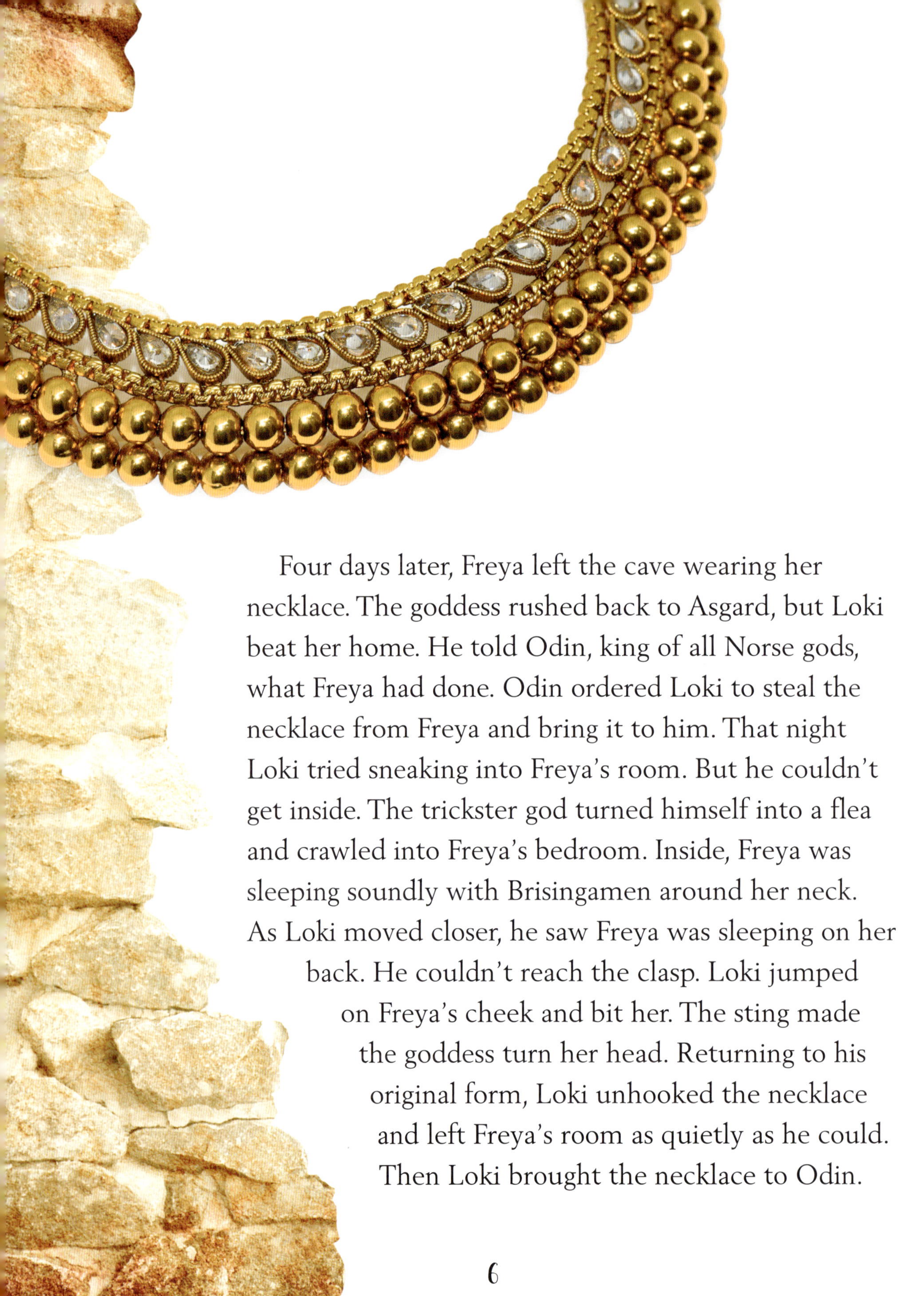

Four days later, Freya left the cave wearing her necklace. The goddess rushed back to Asgard, but Loki beat her home. He told Odin, king of all Norse gods, what Freya had done. Odin ordered Loki to steal the necklace from Freya and bring it to him. That night Loki tried sneaking into Freya's room. But he couldn't get inside. The trickster god turned himself into a flea and crawled into Freya's bedroom. Inside, Freya was sleeping soundly with Brisingamen around her neck. As Loki moved closer, he saw Freya was sleeping on her back. He couldn't reach the clasp. Loki jumped on Freya's cheek and bit her. The sting made the goddess turn her head. Returning to his original form, Loki unhooked the necklace and left Freya's room as quietly as he could. Then Loki brought the necklace to Odin.

The next morning, Freya awoke to find her beloved necklace missing. She knew only Loki could have entered her room without waking her. And Loki wouldn't have done so without Odin's permission. Freya demanded that Odin give her necklace back. Odin agreed, on one condition. Freya must stir up a war between two kings in Midgard, a **realm** connected to Asgard by a massive rainbow bridge. The war would cause great destruction and death for years to come.

realm—a world

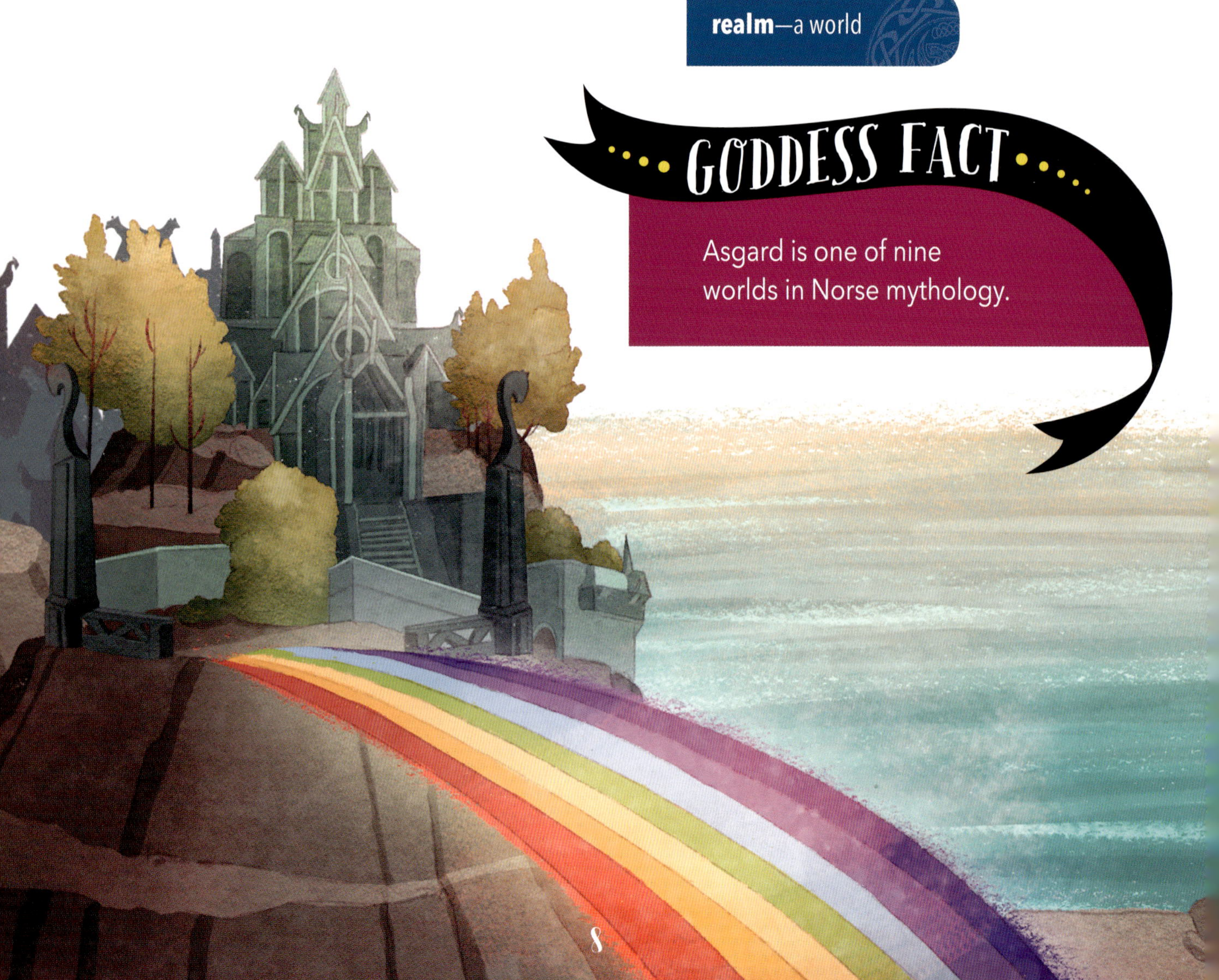

GODDESS FACT

Asgard is one of nine worlds in Norse mythology.

Freya thought hard about Odin's demand and what it would do to humankind. After some time, Freya turned to Odin and said, "Then give me my necklace."

Odin

FREYA OR FRIGGA?

Freya is often linked to another Nordic goddess named Frigga. The two goddesses are quite similar. Both represent beauty. But Freya is usually thought of as a young **maiden** or warrior. Frigga is viewed as a mature wife and mother. Some people believe that Freya and Frigga are the same goddess. Others insist that they are separate beings.

maiden—young, unmarried woman

GODDESS FACT

The name of this goddess is spelled in different ways. The Old Norse spelling is "Freyja." Other spellings include "Freiya," "Fröja," and "Frøya."

Frigga

Chapter 2

FREYA'S MAGIC

The Norse gods belonged to two **tribes**—the Æsir and the Vanir. Freya was from the Vanir tribe. She was known for using a type of magic called seidr. With seidr, Freya could control the weather, bring wealth, and cure illnesses. She could also bring misfortune to others.

Like others who practiced this powerful magic, Freya would often travel from region to region, offering spells for a price. Freya began visiting the Æsir gods in Asgard. Soon they became obsessed with her magic. The Æsir put their desires ahead of their values, laws, and even their own families. The Æsir blamed Freya. They thought she was evil and tried to kill her. They burned her three different times. But each time she rose from the ashes.

tribe—a group of people who share the same language and way of life

GODDESS FACT

Freya and the other Vanir gods are associated with nature, wild animals, and the fairy and spirit realms.

During the war between the tribes, the Æsir fought with weapons. The Vanir used magic.

The Æsir and the Vanir began to fear and hate each other. This led to a great war between the two tribes. The conflict went on for a long time, but neither tribe emerged as the winner. Finally the gods decided to make peace with each other. As part of a peace agreement, a small number of gods and goddesses from each tribe were sent to live with the other group. Freya, her father, Njord, and her twin brother, Freyr, went to live with the Æsir. The Æsir gods Hoenir and Mimir were sent to live with the Vanir.

FREYA TEACHES ODIN

When Freya arrived in Asgard, Odin asked her to teach him seidr. In exchange, he would share the knowledge of the runes with her. The ancient runes were secret magical spells and symbols. Odin treasured this knowledge. Those who knew the runes's magic held great power. Freya agreed to show him seidr. Odin learned to transform into anything he wanted. He could also cast spells. And Odin kept his word. Freya gained the power of the runes.

GODDESS FACT

In 2014 **archaeologists** discovered the ancient grave of a woman in Denmark. Inside, they found a metal wand and a silver, chair-shaped **amulet**. These and other objects suggest the woman was a powerful Norse **shaman**.

Lindholm amulet, a Scandinavian runic charm from around 400 AD

The Magical Art of Seidr

When Freya practiced seidr, she would enter a trance. This allowed her to travel to the spirit world. The spirits would tell her what was destined to happen on Earth.

In ancient Norse society, seidr was largely practiced by women called shamans. People believed that shamans could change a person's destiny. Shamans could use seidr for good and evil. They could heal the sick, bring good fortune, speak to animals and fish, and control the weather. They could also cast curses, cause illnesses, and even kill people. Because of this, shamans were both feared and respected in the ancient world.

archaeologist—a scientist who studies how people lived in the past

amulet—a small charm believed to protect the wearer from harm

shaman—a person who uses magic to cure the sick and control events

Chapter 3

A FAMILY OF GODS

Freya's father was the sea god Njord. He was known for his great wisdom, as well as his love for harbors and boats. Freya's mother was Njord's sister, Nerthus. She was a goddess of **fertility**, as was Freya. In ancient mythology, it was common for gods and goddesses to fall in love with and even marry their siblings. After Njord joined the Æsir, he married a giantess named Skadi.

Freya's twin brother, Freyr, also ruled over fertility and the harvest. In Asgard, Freyr married Gerd, a goddess known for her great beauty. Freyr was worshipped as one of the most important Norse gods. Ancient people believed he could give them a bountiful harvest.

Freyr

Freya married Od when she joined the Æsir in Asgard. Some people believe Od was the god Odin. Freya and Od had two daughters—Hnoss and Gersimi. If Od was Odin, that would make Freya stepmother to Odin's sons, Thor and Loki. Thor was the god of the sky and thunder. Loki was a troublemaker among the gods. His father was the giant Farbauti. But Odin adopted Loki, making him part of the Æsir.

GODDESS FACT

Unlike gods in Greek and Roman mythology, Norse **deities** are **mortal**. They will die one day. Some even meet their end in Norse myths.

fertility—the ability to have children

deity—a god or goddess

mortal—having a lifetime with a beginning and an end

FREYA'S FAMILY TREE

Freya's family consisted of her parents, Njord and Nerthus, and her twin brother Freyr. Later Freya married and had two daughters, Hnoss and Gersimi. She may have been stepmother to the gods Thor and Loki.

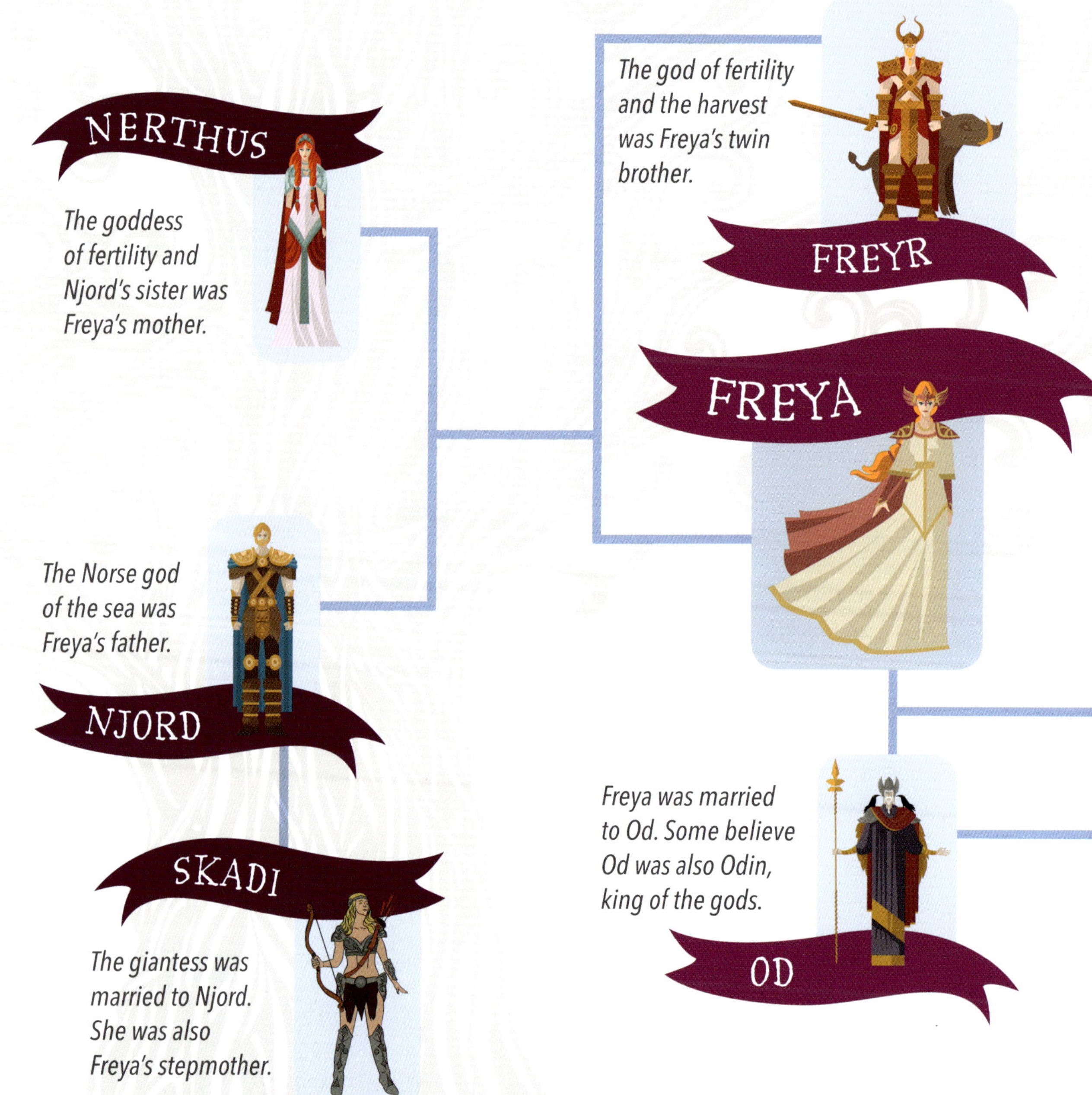

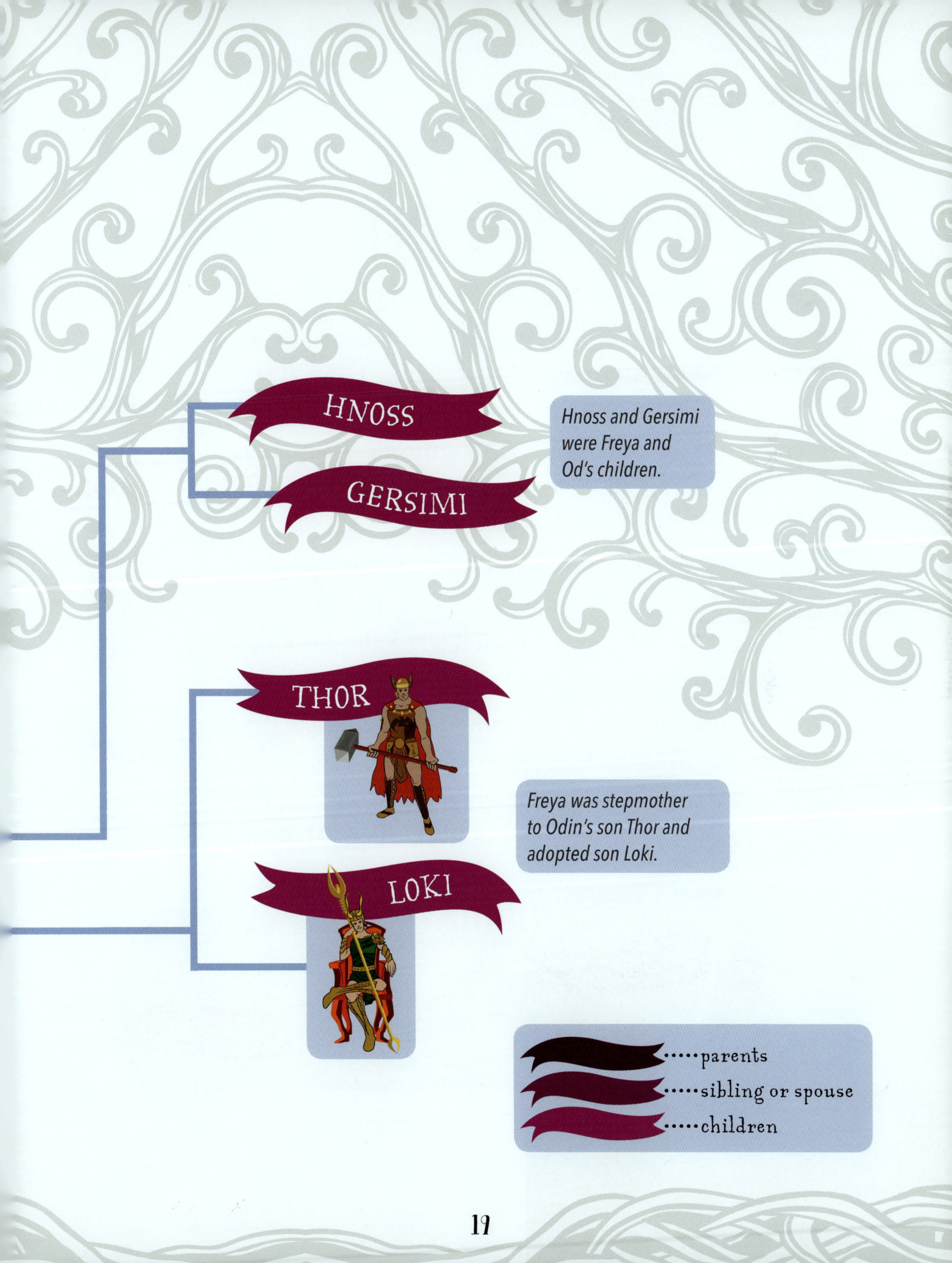
HNOSS
GERSIMI
Hnoss and Gersimi were Freya and Od's children.
THOR
Freya was stepmother to Odin's son Thor and adopted son Loki.
LOKI
parents
sibling or spouse
children

Chapter 4

THE GODDESS'S POWERS

Like many goddesses from Norse mythology, Freya possessed several special powers. Using seidr, she could cast spells and transform into other beings. Freya also had a powerful cloak. It was one of her most valued possessions. Made of falcon feathers, the cloak let Freya fly between worlds. She often lent it to other gods who needed it.

In addition to being the goddess of love and fertility, Freya ruled Folkvangr. This place is in the Norse afterlife. After a battle ended, Freya would select half of the dead heroes and take them to Folkvangr. Then a group of warrior maidens called the Valkyries would take the other half to Valhalla, a place ruled by Odin. The Valkyries are said to create the vibrant colors of the Northern Lights as they fly to and from the battlefields.

GODDESS FACT

The Northern Lights are a natural light display seen in the night skies of the Northern Hemisphere.

GODDESS FACT

Freya traveled on a **chariot** pulled by two blue cats. The cats were given to her by Thor.

chariot—a light, two-wheeled cart pulled by animals

In modern art and literature, Freya wears a Viking helmet. The Vikings were ancient Norse warriors who sailed between Scandinavia and Europe from the 800s to 1000s. They were known for violently raiding other lands.

model of an ancient Viking ship

THOR AND FREYA

One morning, Thor woke up to find that his mighty hammer was missing. Thrym, the king of the Frost Giants, had stolen it. Thor's brother Loki rushed to Freya and asked to borrow her special cloak. The magical item would take him to the land of the giants. Wanting to help Thor, Freya agreed.

When Loki arrived in the land of the giants, he confronted Thrym. The giant king admitted to stealing Thor's hammer. But Thrym had put the hammer deep in the earth. No one could retrieve it but him. The giant king told Loki he would give Thor's hammer back on one condition—Freya had to marry him.

Loki flew back to Asgard and told Freya what Thrym had said. The goddess was furious. The ground shook with her anger. Freya would never be traded as someone's prize. She refused to marry someone she didn't know.

All the gods and goddesses in Asgard gathered to discuss how to get Thor's hammer back. It was decided that Thor would dress in a wedding gown and pose as Freya. The god of thunder covered his face with a veil. Freya even lent him her beloved Brisingamen necklace.

The plan worked. Thrym welcomed his bride into the land of the giants. By the time Thrym realized he had been tricked, Thor had retrieved his hammer. Then Thor killed Thrym and the other giants.

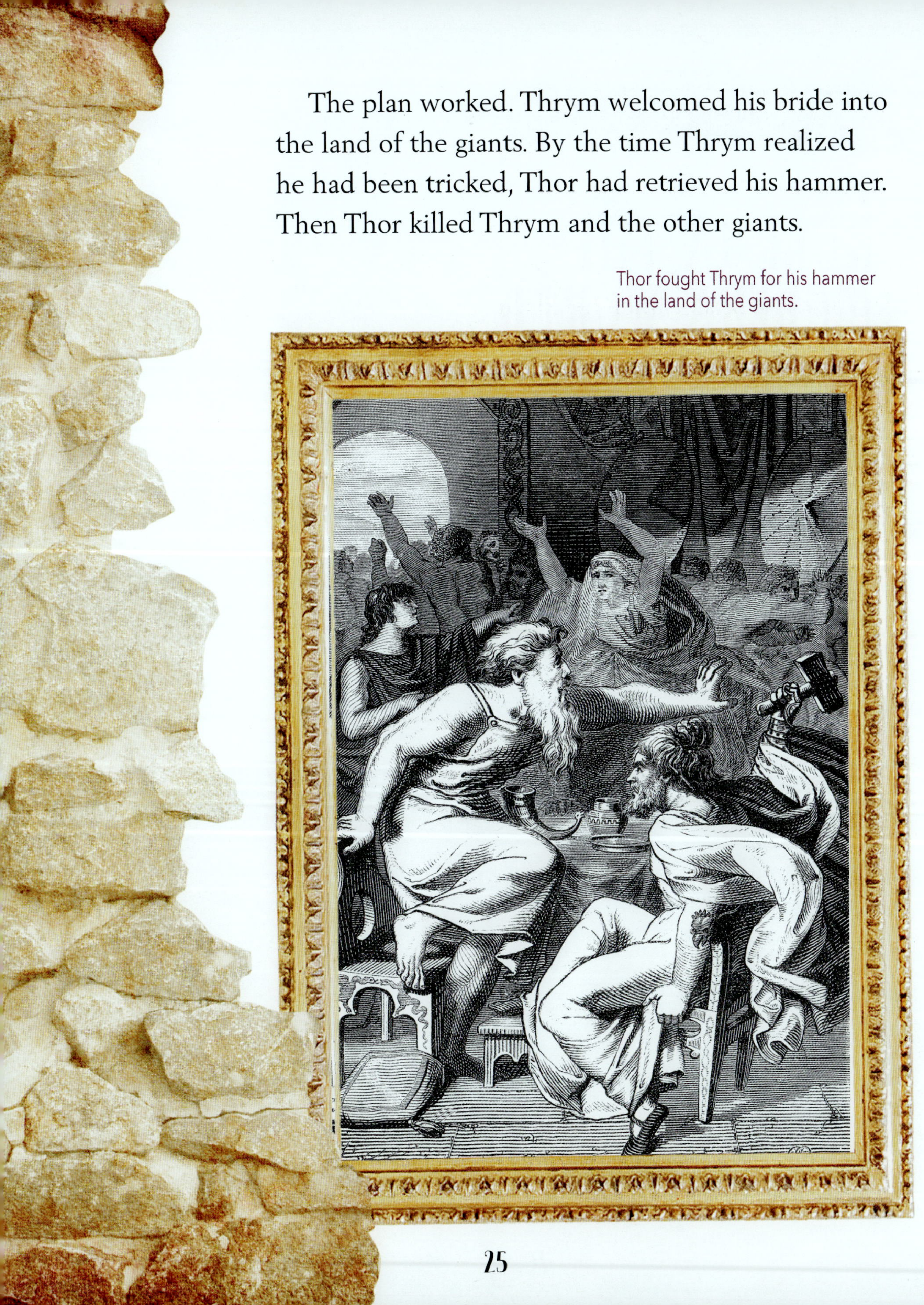

Thor fought Thrym for his hammer in the land of the giants.

Chapter 5

ROLE IN THE MODERN WORLD

Ancient mythology remains an important part of many cultures today. Some people view the Norse myths as entertaining stories with meaningful lessons. But others take them more seriously. They see them as links to the past and part of world history. Stories about Freya and the other Norse deities have inspired artists, writers, and TV and movie makers.

GODDESS FACT

Today, Freya's followers pray to her during the full moon. They believe the moon is one of her symbols.

Freya is **worshipped** by certain groups today. In Denmark, as many as 1,000 people follow the Norse deities. Women who wish to have children pray to Freya for help.

People in Denmark, Norway, and Sweden name their infant daughters after Freya. During the 2000s, the name "Freya" became popular in the United Kingdom. In recent years, it has also gained popularity in the United States.

Authors such as Neil Gaiman have written books about Norse mythology. In Gaiman's 2017 book *Norse Mythology*, the author retells many of the original stories. It became a *New York Times* bestseller.

worship—to express love and devotion to a god

A statue of Freya is in Stockholm, Sweden.

FREYA IN *POP* CULTURE

Marvel's *Thor* comic books have introduced Freya and her myths to a new audience. In recent years, the *Thor* films have also brought Freya, Thor, Loki, and other Norse deities into popular culture. Freya appears in the first *Thor* movie as Frigga, played by Rene Russo.

Rene Russo as Frigga

Wednesday, Thursday, Freya?

The days of the week were named after the Norse gods. Some believe that Freya or Frigga inspired Friday. Others think the day was named after Freya's brother, Freyr.

GODDESS FACT

Freya is often compared to the Greek goddess Aphrodite and the Roman goddess Venus.

Aphrodite

GLOSSARY

amulet (AM-yoo-let)—a small charm believed to protect the wearer from harm

archaeologist (ar-kee-AH-luh-jist)—a scientist who studies how people lived in the past

chariot (CHAYR-ee-uht)—a light, two-wheeled cart pulled by animals

deity (DEE-uh-tee)—a god or goddess

fertility (fur-TIL-uh-tee)—the ability to have children

forge (FORJ)—a place where metal is melted and molded into various objects

maiden (MAYD-uhn)—young, unmarried woman

mortal (MOR-tuhl)—having a lifetime with a beginning and an end

realm (RELM)—a world

shaman (SHAH-mehn)—a person who uses magic to cure the sick and control events

tribe (TRIBE)—a group of people who share the same language and way of life

worship (WUR-ship)—to express love and devotion to a god

READ MORE

Alexander, Heather. *A Child's Introduction to Norse Mythology: Odin, Thor, Loki, and Other Viking Gods, Goddesses, Giants, and Monsters*. New York: Black Dog & Leventhal, 2018.

Braun, Eric. *Norse Myths*. Mythology Around the World. North Mankato, MN: Capstone Press, 2018.

Loh-Hagan, Virginia. *Freya*. Gods and Goddesses of the Ancient World. Ann Arbor, MI: Cherry Lake Publishing, 2018.

INTERNET SITES

The Vikings Gods and Myths
https://vikings.mrdonn.org/gods.html

Viking Gods
https://www.dkfindout.com/us/history/vikings/viking-gods/

INDEX